PIANO   VOCAL   GUITAR

the sing-off songbook

ISBN 978-1-4584-0652-1

HAL•LEONARD®
CORPORATION
7777 W. BLUEMOUND RD. P.O. BOX 13819 MILWAUKEE, WI 53213

Visit Hal Leonard Online at
www.halleonard.com

APOLOGIZE

Words and Music by
RYAN TEDDER

BABY

Words and Music by JUSTIN BIEBER,
CHRISTOPHER STEWART, CHRISTINE FLORES,
CHRISTOPHER BRIDGES and TERIUS NASH

COOLER THAN ME

Words and Music by MIKE POSNER
and ERIC HOLLJES

26

CREEP

Words and Music by ALBERT HAMMOND,
MIKE HAZLEWOOD, THOMAS YORKE,
RICHARD GREENWOOD, PHILIP SELWAY,
COLIN GREENWOOD and EDWARD O'BRIAN

FINAL COUNTDOWN

Words and Music by
JOEY TEMPEST

Moderately

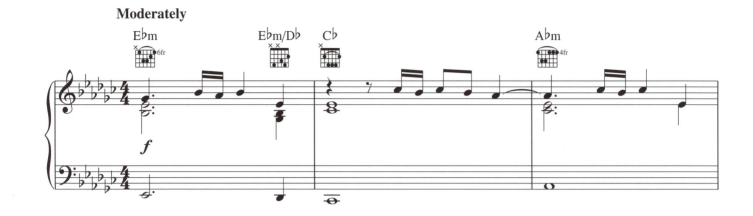

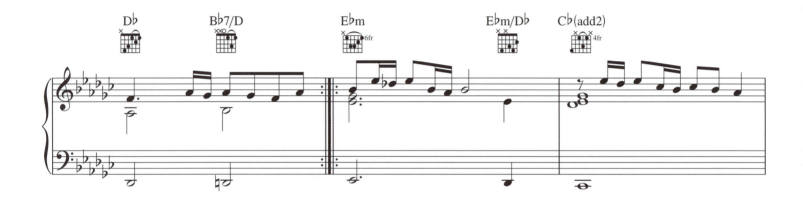

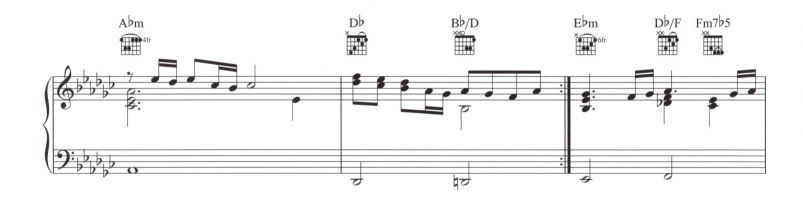

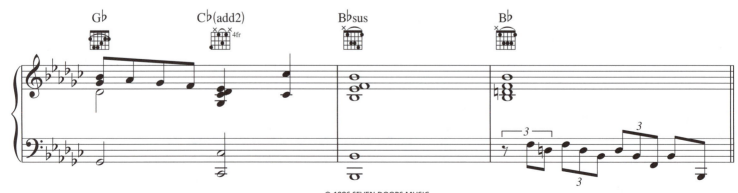

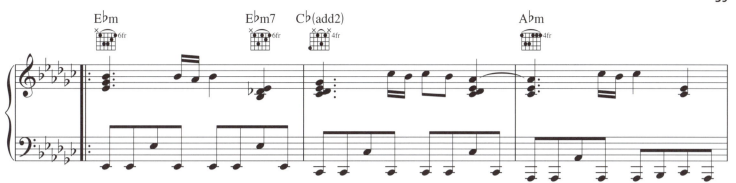

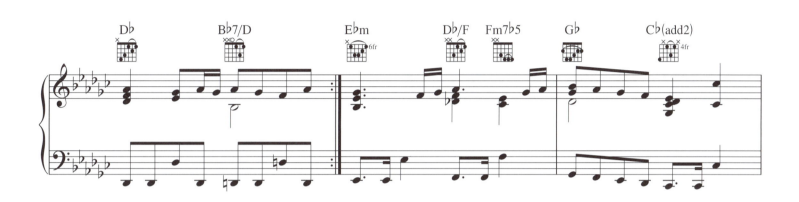

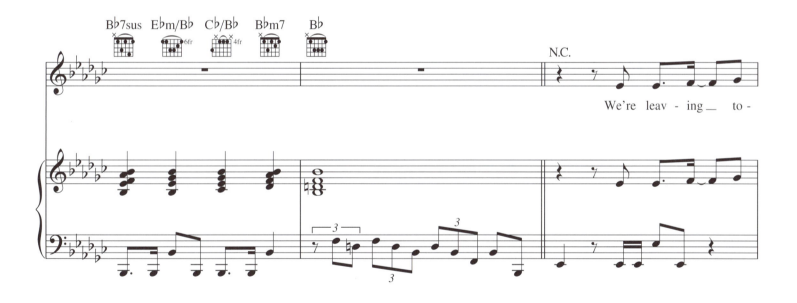

We're leav - ing __ to -

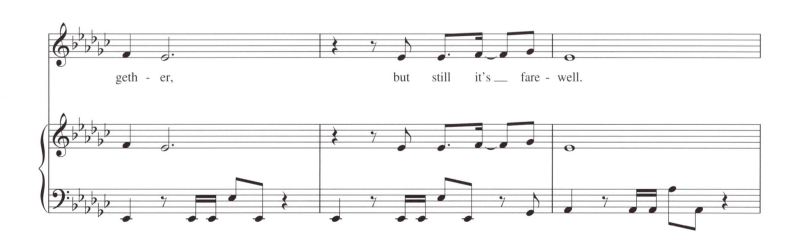

geth - er,   but still it's __ fare - well.

I'VE GOT THE MUSIC IN ME

Words and Music by
BIAS BOSHELL

Moderately

Ain't got no trou-bles in my ____ life.

No fool-ish dreams to make me ____ cry. I'm nev-er fright-ened or wor-

-ried; I know I'll al-ways ____ get by. I get up,

GOOD GIRLS GO BAD

Words and Music by GABE SAPORTA,
KARA DioGUARDI, KEVIN RUDOLF
and J. KASH

GRACE KELLY

Words and Music by MIKA,
JODI MARR, JOHN MERCHANT
and DAN WARNER

I STILL HAVEN'T FOUND WHAT I'M LOOKING FOR

Words by BONO and THE EDGE
Music by U2

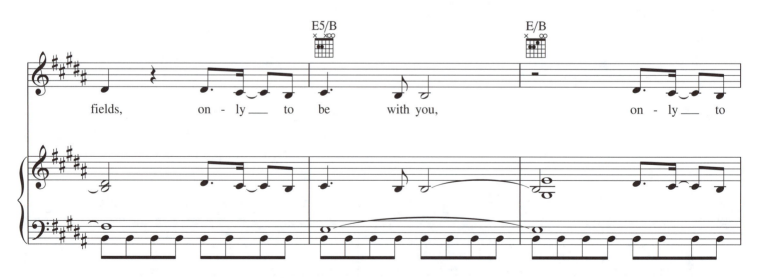

LANDSLIDE

Words and Music by
STEVIE NICKS

Moderately fast

I took my love ___ ___ and I took it down. ___ I climbed a moun - tain and I ___ turned ___

* *Lead vocal written one octave higher than sung.*

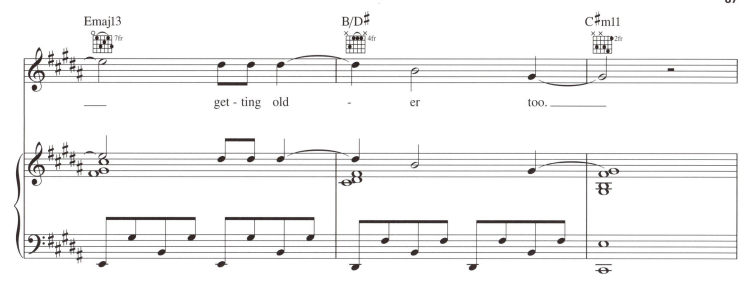

get - ting old - er too.

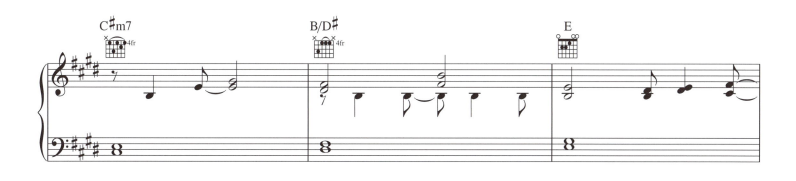

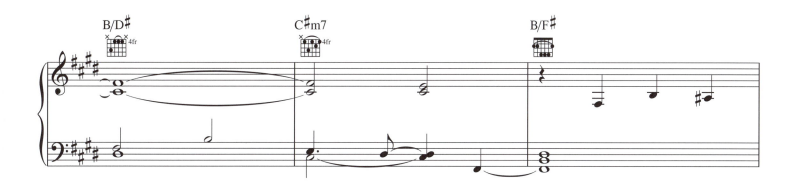

MERCY

Words and Music by AIMEE DUFFY
and STEPHEN BOOKER

MR. BLUE SKY

Words and Music by
JEFF LYNNE

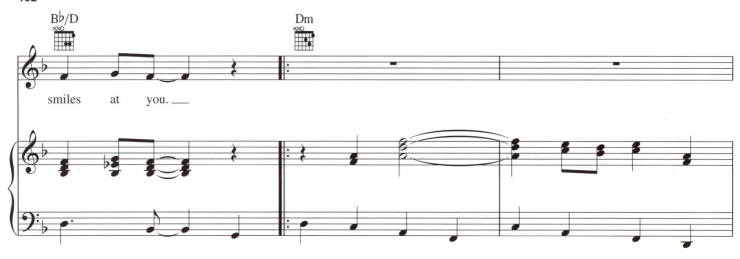

smiles at you. ___

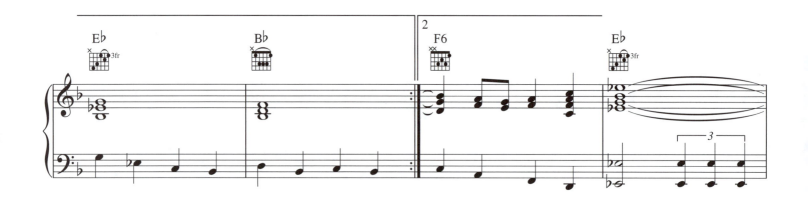

PUT A LITTLE LOVE IN YOUR HEART

Words and Music by JIMMY HOLIDAY,
RANDY MYERS and JACKIE DeSHANNON

104

21 GUNS

Words and Music by DAVID BOWIE,
JOHN PHILLIPS, BILLIE JOE ARMSTRONG,
MIKE PRITCHARD and FRANK WRIGHT

UNDER PRESSURE

Words and Music by FREDDIE MERCURY,
JOHN DEACON, BRIAN MAY,
ROGER TAYLOR and DAVID BOWIE

USE SOMEBODY

Words and Music by CALEB FOLLOWILL,
NATHAN FOLLOWILL, JARED FOLLOWILL
and MATTHEW FOLLOWILL

WITH A LITTLE HELP FROM MY FRIENDS

Words and Music by JOHN LENNON
and PAUL McCARTNEY

What would you do ____ if I sang

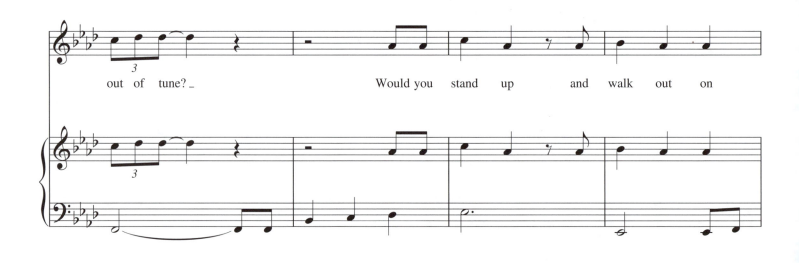

out of tune? ____ Would you stand up and walk out on

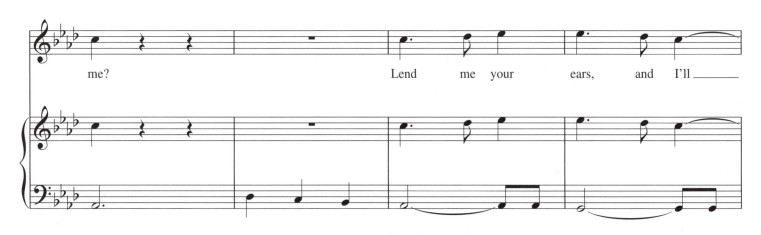

me? Lend me your ears, and I'll ____

TAKE A BOW

Words and Music by SHAFFER SMITH,
TOR ERIK HERMANSEN and MIKKEL ERIKSEN